Artists at Work

Clay

Cheryl Jakab

Smart Apple Media

This edition first published in 2006 in the United States of America by Smart Apple Media.

Smart Apple Media
2140 Howard Drive West
North Mankato
Minnesota 56003

First published in 2006 by
MACMILLAN EDUCATION AUSTRALIA PTY LTD
627 Chapel Street, South Yarra, Australia 3141

Visit our Web site at www.macmillan.com.au

Associated companies and representatives throughout the world.

Library of Congress Cataloging-in-Publication Data

Jakab, Cheryl.
  Clay / by Cheryl Jakab.
  p. cm.—(Artists at work)
  Includes index.
  ISBN-13: 978-1-58340-775-2
  1. Pottery—Juvenile literature. I. Title.

  NK4240.J25 2006
  738.1—dc22   2005056775

Edited by Sam Munday
Text and cover design by Karen Young
Page layout by Karen Young
Photo research by Jes Senbergs
Illustrations by Ann Likhovetsky

Printed in USA

Acknowledgments
The author would like to acknowledge and thank all the working artists and hobbyists who have been quoted, appear, or assisted in creating this book.

The author and the publisher are grateful to the following for permission to reproduce copyright material:

Cover photograph: Woman making pottery, courtesy of Amos Nachoum/CORBIS.

Australian Ceramics Directory, p. 22; Wedgwood vase, c.1780 (jasperware), Flaxman, John (1755-1826)/ Hanley Museum & Art Gallery, Staffordshire, UK/Bridgeman Art Library p. 16 (bottom); Ceramics Australia, p. 26; Coo-ee Picture Library, pp. 4 (right), 6, 8 (middle), 20, 23; Corbis, pp. 5, 7 (right), 9, 10 (top), 11, 12, 13, 15, 16 (top), 17, 18, 21, 25; Rob Cruse, pp. 4 (1), 24; Getty Images pp. 4 (top), 10 (bottom), 14; Image Library, p. 8 (top and bottom); Istockphoto, p. 7 (left); Cheryl Jakab, p. 27; Photolibrary.com, p. 19.

While every care has been taken to trace and acknowledge copyright, the publisher tenders their apologies for any accidental infringement where copyright has proved untraceable. Where the attempt has been unsuccessful, the publisher welcomes information that would redress the situation.

Please note
At the time of printing, the Internet addresses appearing in this book were correct. Owing to the dynamic nature of the Internet, however, we cannot guarantee that all these addresses will remain correct.

Contents

Glossary words

When a word is printed in **bold**, you can look up its meaning in the Glossary on page 31.

Clay artists

Look at these different artworks made by clay artists. People who design and make artworks with clay are called potters or ceramic artists. Ceramic artists make a wide variety of items including:

- **adobe** houses, **kilns**, and furniture
- terracotta pots, tiles, and figures
- fine **porcelain** and **bone china** tableware and **figurines**
- abstract ceramic sculptures
- **glazed** floor tiles and furniture
- **stoneware** and **earthenware** cups, mugs, and pots

Glazing helps to make all kinds of clay artworks look attractive.

Some bone china artworks can be used in the home.

Not all clay artworks have colors added to them.

4

Using clay

Clay artists are very skilled at choosing, shaping, decorating, and firing clay. In this book, you will find the answers to these questions and more:

- ● What would it be like to work as a ceramic artist?

- ● What is it that potters like about clay as a **medium** for their art?

- ● How does clay help express artistic ideas?

- ● What do you need to know about clay to work it?

"Joy lies in store for anyone who chooses to work with clay."
Peter Cosentino, ceramic artist, teacher, and author

▲ Clay artists develop skill in shaping clay.

5

What is clay?

Clay is a kind of mud that can be molded when it gets wet. Clay forms from the tiniest grains of mineral from worn rocks. The crystals in clay have a structure which allows them to hold water. Moist clay is said to be very plastic, which means it can be easily shaped. When heated to high temperatures, it changes to become hard and **impermeable**.

The main types of useful clays are called kaolinites, formed from the mineral aluminum silicate. There are many different types of kaolinite clay used by artists including terracotta, adobe, and china clay. Clay may be white, grey, red, yellow, blue, or black depending on the combinations of minerals in it. Each type of clay has different characteristics.

◀ Clay is removed from the earth in mines or quarries.

Types of clay

Type of clay	Characteristics	Uses
adobe	• fine mixture of clay, **quartz,** and other minerals	• mixed with straw to make bricks for houses in areas of low rainfall
china clay	• white and fine • made up of very small particles	• stoneware or fine objects
fireclay	• white, very fine clay • must be fired in high temperatures	• used in bricks for fireplaces or ovens • pots for glass working
vitrifiable clay	• mixture of minerals with china clay • turns glassy when fired	• porcelain china
terracotta	• coarse clay • turns from buff to dark red earthenware when fired	• pots, statues, and bricks

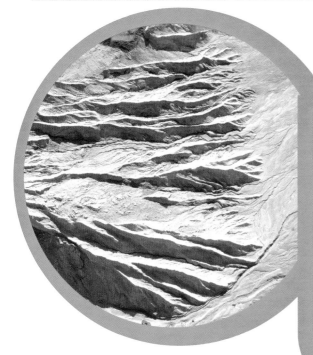

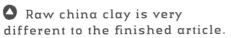 Raw china clay is very different to the finished article.

Clay work

Potters use the range of clays available to create different ceramic products. The word "ceramic" comes from the ancient Greek word "keramikos" after an area in ancient Greece that produced pottery. The minerals in clay become ceramic when heated to high temperatures. The way the final product looks depends on both the type of clay and how it is made.

Ceramic types

Type of ceramic	Temperature of firing (degrees Farenheit/°F)	Characteristics	Uses and history
Earthenware	lowest kiln temperatures 1652–2192°F (900–1200°C)	• must be glazed to be waterproof • colored buff, red, brown, or black	• household dinnerware • all ancient, medieval, Middle Eastern, and European painted ceramics
Stoneware	medium kiln temperatures 2192–2336°F (1200–1280°C)	• durable • waterproof • colored white, buff, gray, or red	• heavy cooking pots • first used in ancient China
Porcelain	highest kiln temperatures 2282–2372°F (1250–1300°C)	• resonant and **translucent** material • great density and hardness • colored white	• fine dinnerware • first made by the Chinese in the 700s A.D.

Obtaining clay

Most potters today do not dig up their own clay, although it is possible to do so. Most potters select and buy clay from suppliers.

Shaping clay

Clay can be molded into a wide range of shapes and structures with the right techniques. Some clay workers build by hand while others use machines such as pottery wheels to help them.

Decorating

Many decorating techniques have been developed including coloring, painting, imprinting, cutting, and glazing.

Drying and firing

Once heated in a kiln, the worked clay hardens and holds its shape. The only risk to it lasting virtually forever is that it is brittle. It will break if dropped or hit by a hard object.

⬤ Many shaped clay artworks can be fired in a kiln at the same time.

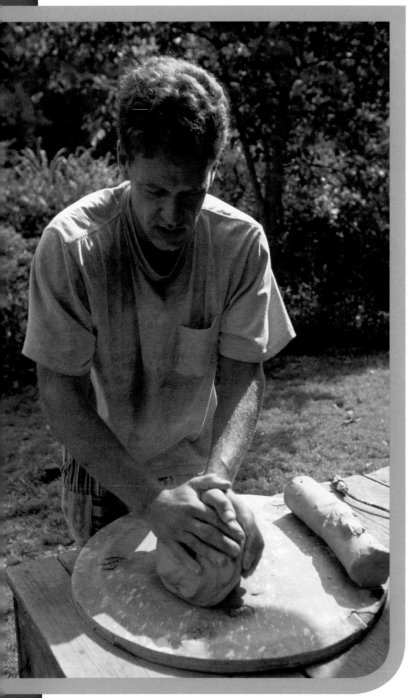

Designing with clay

When designing with clay, the artist needs to think about the type of clay, processes, and decorations to use. Each type of clay, such as fine porcelain and stoneware, creates very different products and effects. Different styles, forms, and finishes suit different purposes and can go in and out of fashion.

Advantages of working with clay

Clay has one great advantage over other artist's mediums. Just about any shape that the artist imagines can be formed from clay. Clay is easily shaped and reshaped. It holds its shape after firing, when it becomes as hard as rock.

⬤⬤⬤ Clay allows the artist to create unusual shapes with their artwork.

▲ Coloring a clay artwork can add character to it.

Coloring

Color can be added to clay by:

- ▶ mixing it with the raw clay
- ▶ painting or spraying color on dry forms
- ▶ adding it to a glaze
- ▶ painting or spraying color after glazing

The Artist Speaks

"Styles and tastes in pottery are constantly changing."
**Peter Cosentino,
potter and teacher**

Hand building

Hand building is the most ancient method of shaping clay and is still popular today. Whether the artist is creating a huge terracotta figure or a fine porcelain jug, there are a few basic steps that must be followed.

Kneading

Kneading is necessary to make the clay soft and **pliable** for shaping. It can be done by hand or machine. Kneading helps to get rid of air pockets in the clay and remove any hard lumps that may affect the final product.

Shaping

Techniques for shaping clay include pinching, coiling, press molding, and slab construction.

Decorating

Shaped clay can be left plain or the surface can be changed in some way. Methods of decorating include pressing patterns and shapes into the damp clay, cutting, coloring, combing, and applying extra clay.

▶ Decorating clay can take time.

▶ Heat can be used to speed up the drying process.

Drying

After shaping, the damp clay needs to dry gradually so that it does not crack. Drying may need to be sped up or slowed down depending on the weather, the size of the object, and the type of clay. Placing a damp cloth over the item slows the drying process.

Firing

When the object has dried it is placed in a pottery kiln for firing. The kiln is slowly heated to the right temperature, which varies with the type of clay used. This changes soft clay into hard ceramic.

Glazing

Many wonderful colors and effects are created with glazes. Coatings can be applied before or after firing. Glaze is often applied after a first low firing. The object is then fired again to a higher temperature to make the glaze hard and waterproof.

The Artist Speaks

"A well made ceramic piece should be balanced in form and be pleasing to the eye."
Tracey McMurray, potter

Clay history

▼ Fragments of ancient pottery can tell us a lot about clay history.

Shaping, decorating, and firing pottery are skills that have developed over thousands of years. By 3000 B.C. many cultures were making fired clay pots and decorating them.

The development of very fine clay objects began in Asia. In the 600s and 700s A.D., the Chinese began mixing minerals to make porcelain. About 500 years ago, kaolin was discovered and mixed into china clay to make the porcelain that we know today.

Lead-glazed earthenware became popular in Europe during the 1500s and 1600s. English stoneware was made on a large scale only after the late 1600s. It was not until the early 1700s that Europeans were able to reproduce fine ceramics.

The Artist Speaks

"The pottery fragment may be worth looking at—for it may have a story to tell."
Tony Birks, potter

Great clay traditions

Evidence from early Chinese, Greek, and Japanese cultures show that each developed its own traditions and skills with ceramics.

Chinese celadon

Classic Chinese celadon items are among the greatest ceramic works ever made. Celadon is a porcelain-like stoneware produced in China, Korea, Japan, and Thailand. The glaze resembles jade, which is highly valued in the East. The popularity of celadon in east Asia was due partly to superstition. It was believed that celadon containers would break or change color if poison was put in them.

⬢ This is a later example of Chinese celadon, dating from 1725.

The first celadon called Yue (or green ware) appeared in China around 220 A.D. Green ware is made of simple yet elegant shapes. Celadon techniques were developed further in the next few hundred years. The art was at its most popular in the 1100s during the Song dynasty. Examples from these times are now very rare and extremely valuable.

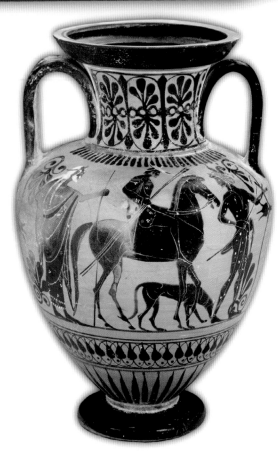

This Greek black figure pot is over 2,600 years old.

The greatest clay treasures come from throughout history and from across the globe.

Greek black figure pots

In approximately 675 B.C., painters in Corinth, Greece began to decorate vases with black figures in silhouette. Many examples of these detailed glazed ceramics show great skill. The vases are often decorated with monsters, such as a fire-breathing creature with a lion's head, a goat's body, and a serpent's tail.

English jasperware

Jasperware was a stoneware that Englishman Josiah Wedgwood developed in 1774. Wedgwood became known for his finely-made cream-coloured earthenware. This led to him being appointed "royal supplier of dinnerware" in 1762. Wedgwood developed many revolutionary ceramic materials. He was also involved in perfecting **slipcasting** at the end of the 1700s. His jasperware was the earliest example of slipcasting, which makes it highly treasured.

This Wedgwood jasperware vase was designed by John Flaxman around 1780.

Jomon pottery

Some of the world's earliest pottery comes from the Jomon period (10 000–300 B.C.) in Japan. Jomon is highly treasured because it is so old. Most other ancient cultures did not fire pottery until farming was developed. The Jomon period is named after the twisted cord decorations made on clay pots.

First ceramic sculptures

The first ceramic sculptures were made by the Jomon people around 2500 B.C. They were figurines called *dogu*. The purpose of these figurines is still debated. Some people believe the figurines were dolls for children.

▲ Dogu figurines are the world's oldest surviving ceramic artworks.

CASE STUDY
Terracotta Army

The largest set of ceramic figures ever created is known as the Terracotta Army. This amazingly well-preserved collection includes 6,000 life-size statues of soldiers and horses made in terracotta clay. It was discovered in March 1974 at Qin, near the modern city of Xi'an in China. Each figure is individually modeled to look like a different person.

The Terracotta Army was part of the burial tomb of the first Qin emperor of China, who had the Great Wall of China built. The tomb was built approximately 2,100 years ago. Ancient Chinese writings tell us that the underground tomb contained a vast palace to house the dead emperor.

▶ Each figure in the Terracotta Army is decorated in great detail.

The Terracotta Army is a popular tourist attraction in Xi'an.

Where clay artists work

Clay artists need a special workspace. Working with clay can be very messy, so the workspace is usually away from other living areas. The clay artist's working space should be large, light, and airy with running water. If the artist fires their own works, then they also need an area for a kiln. Kilns require safe conditions and a fuel source such as gas or electricity.

The pottery wheel is an important piece of equipment in the clay artists' workshop.

Space is needed to house all the clay, clay-working tools (such as a pottery wheel), and shelves to dry items on. The workshop also needs to house many hand tools that assist with the process of working the clay. Many of these are made of wood but can be very sharp and need to be kept in a safe place.

CASE STUDY
Clay kilns

Kilns are used to fire clay items. Kilns must be raised to the temperatures required to turn the clay objects into ceramics. The earliest kilns were fired by wood but today they can also be fuelled by gas and electricity. The size of the kiln used depends on the size and volume of the product.

Baking ceramics

Firing ceramics is like baking food, except ceramics "cook" at higher temperatures. When using a kiln, small clay cones are placed inside to show when the kiln has received enough heat. When these cones slump, the potter knows the kiln has reached the correct temperature.

🔺 Some kilns are built outside the workshop for safety reasons.

Showing clay artworks

The Australian Ceramics Directory was launched in 2002.

It is important for clay artists to show and sell their work. They can show the works they make through exhibitions, competitions, markets, shops, galleries, and Web sites. The public can then see the works that the artists design and make. The artists must show their work in places that make it easy for the public to see them.

Online Web sites allow ceramic artists wider public exposure and are a good way of exhibiting work. Online information and images can be updated regularly and they provide interested people with greater detail and faster access than was possible in the past.

◀ Groups such as The Potters Society of Australia are often contacted for information about Australian ceramic artists.

Making a living as an artist

Ceramic artists have to sell their artworks in order to be able to continue working on their pieces. Some artists may sell examples of their work in shops or markets, or teach their art at schools and colleges. Public art galleries may purchase artworks to keep and display in their public collections.

Commissioned work

Sometimes artists work by commission. This means they are asked to create a particular type of artwork for a client and are paid to do the job.

In 1993, Giuseppi Raneri was commissioned to make artworks to place in the streets near his ceramics studio and shop which was then located in Melbourne, Australia. He decided to create three concrete benches covered by painted, glazed ceramic tiles.

"The works had to be practical as well as artistic. We had no idea if people would use them."
Giuseppi Raneri, ceramic artist

🔻 "Fiesta" by Raneri represents a party atmosphere. It is bright and sunny.

Clay artists' groups

Clay artists' groups share ideas and organize meetings for artists to learn more about their craft. At such events there are usually exhibitions, talks, and practical demonstrations. In 2004, Jingdezhen in China hosted the 1,000 Years Celebration of Porcelain where visitors learned techniques of classic porcelain production. This area of China has produced the finest porcelain for more than 1,000 years.

In 2004, a week-long festival of claywork was held in Gulgong in New South Wales, Australia. Gulgong is an area where useful clays are found. Large numbers of potters and international artists were invited to attend and gave workshops.

The Gulgong Clay Modern festival brought many clay artists together.

Issues for clay artists

Clay artists need to be aware of health, safety, and environmental issues that can affect their work.

Health and safety

Health and safety issues when working with clay include problems with dust particles and the dangers of using glazes. Some glazes can be poisonous, so they should be kept away from food. Some glaze chemicals can create dangerous fumes or damage skin. Safety when firing kilns is a critical issue. The heat involved can be dangerous if not handled properly. There is a lot to learn, so many new clay artists rely on experts to do their firings. Most ceramic artists work hard to develop skills in all aspects of ceramic work. This includes the firing which has a significant effect on the final product.

The Artist Speaks

"Fortunately, a clean, careful, and intelligent routine overcomes the risks."
Frank Harmer, author and potter

⬇ Firing can be dangerous if you are not aware of the safety issues.

CASE STUDY
Clay chemistry

The many different types of clay are made from many different types of chemicals found in the soil. The clays of China and England have a long history. They have been explored long enough for potters to have discovered a great deal about their chemistry. Today, new sources of clay are being explored, particularly in countries such as Australia where clay artwork only has a short history.

Many potters are exploring the chemistry of these clays to learn more about how they behave. Any new clay deposit must have its chemistry explored. This allows users of clays to know exactly how a clay will work and fire. Ceramic engineers and **geologists** are among the many people interested in learning more about the chemistry of clay and ceramics.

▶ Knowing about the chemistry of clay means impressive artworks can be created, such as this huge porcelain pot.

◀ Test pieces are used to find out more about the clay, firing, and glazes.

Prospecting for clay

Looking for clay is called prospecting. Some artists now look for their own clay deposits, which may have the right combination of minerals to make ceramics. Clay forms from weathered rock materials. The clay produced varies with the type of **parent rock**. Geological maps showing the rock types of areas can be helpful in locating useful clay deposits. Workable clays that artists can use often have a mixture of minerals in them.

Testing clay

Once a clay deposit has been found, the clay is tested to see if it is suitable for use. The clay is tested by seeing how easily it can be worked by hand and how it changes color when fired. Some clays crack, break, slump, or do not hold shape. Clays that are very plastic and easily worked may shrink and crack in firing. Looking into the chemistry of clay is an important part of a clay artist's work.

PROJECT
Make a decorated clay seal

What you need:

- a block of clay

- rolling pin

- water

- a cutting tool

- smoothing tools

- objects to press on the clay, such as rope, toy wheels, cookie cutters, twigs, stones, and leaves

Clay can be decorated while it is still soft and workable. There are no rules for imprinting in clay, so the possibilities are almost endless. You could try pressing rope into the surface. One small imprint may not look right, but a regular pattern can be very impressive.

Many ancient cultures made **clay seals** from soft, damp clay. They were decorated in many ways that would create a pattern or tiny scene.

Hint: Experiment with imprints made by different objects before you make the final product. You will also need to find someone to fire your seal.

What to do:

1. Knead and roll the clay to a soft lump with no air bubbles. You should use water to stop the clay from drying out.

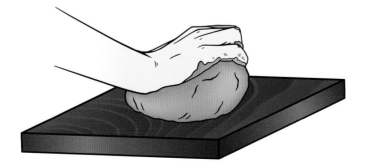

2. Press the clay flat onto a clean surface such as a strong table or bench.

3. Roll out the clay using the rolling pin.

4. Cut out the shape you want to make from the clay.

5. Make your design by pressing your chosen objects onto the clay. The surface can be smoothed and polished or left raw.

Clay timeline

10 000 Jomon period begins in Japan

7000 Early pottery shaped by coiling

5000+ Pottery firing begins

3500+ Pottery wheel first used

2500 Jomon clay sculptures created

2000 Pottery sealed by glazing, allowing oils and milk to be stored in pots

1400 Stoneware produced in China

600s Greek black figure pots made

300 Pottery wheel develops into a heavy disc that keeps spinning for some time

100 Terracotta Army made in China

220 Celadon stoneware produced in China

600–700 Porcelain produced in China using china clay and felspar rock

1575 Soft paste porcelain produced in Italy

1710 Hard paste porcelain produced in Europe

1745 Pottery produced in England by "slipcasting"

1762 Wedgwood made royal supplier of dinnerware in England

around 1800 Bone china produced in Europe

1858 Modern kiln patented in Europe by Frederick Hoffman

1900s Plates and other ceramics shaped by machines using Hoffman's kilns

Glossary

adobe clay made by drying and hardening by the heat of the sun

bone china fine ceramic made with the addition of bone

clay seals pieces of clay with patterns or pictures on them

earthenware pottery fired at low temperatures, which must be glazed to be waterproof

figurines small sculpted figures

geologists scientists who study rocks

glazed a glassy cover or finish

impermeable does not allow fluids to pass through

kilns furnaces or ovens used for firing pottery

medium material used

parent rock rock which eroded to form minerals from which clay is formed

pliable easily bent

porcelain fine, light ceramic that allows light to pass through

quartz a common mineral

slipcasting a method of making a ceramic by allowing a thin film of clay called slip to solidify in a mold

stoneware a glassy ceramic that does not allow light to pass through

translucent allows some light to pass through

Index